The *Shakespeare Library*

Romeo and Juliet

WENDY GREENHILL

HEAD OF EDUCATION,
ROYAL SHAKESPEARE COMPANY

Heinemann Library
Chicago, Illinois

© 2000 Reed Educational & Professional Publishing
Published by Heinemann Library,
an imprint of Reed Educational & Professional Publishing,
100 N. LaSalle, Suite 1010
Chicago, IL 60602
Customer Service 888-454-2279
Visit our website at www.heinemannlibrary.com

Designed by Green Door Design
Printed in Hong Kong

04 03 02 01 00
10 9 8 7 6 5 4 3 2 1

Library of Congress Cataloging-in-Publication Data
Greenhill, Wendy, 1949-
    Romeo and Juliet / Wendy Greenhill.
      p. cm. – (The Shakespeare library)
    Includes bibliographical references (c.) and index.
    Summary: A synopsis of the plot and analysis of the characters in Romeo &
Juliet, an exploration of possible sources of inspiration, and a history of the play's
production.
    ISBN 1-57572-285-2 (lib. bdg.)
    1. Shakespeare, William, 1564-1616. Romeo and Juliet—Juvenile literature. 2.
Tragedy—Juvenile literature. [1. Shakespeare, William, 1564-1616. Romeo and Juliet.
2. English literature—History and criticism.] I. Title: Romeo and Juliet. II. Title.
PR2831.G743 2000
822.3'3—dc21
                                                              99-055123

Acknowledgments
The authors and publishers would like to thank the following for permission
to reproduce photographs and other illustrative material:

Bridgeman Art Library, p. 6; The British Library, p. 4; Cambridge University Library, p. 7;
Photostage/Donald Cooper, pp. 9, 15, 16; E.T. Archive, pp. 5, 26; RSC Collection, pp, 19, 23, 30;
Shakespeare Centre Library/Joe Cocks Studio Collection, pp. 8, 10, 11, 13, 17, 20, 21, 25,
27, 29, 31; Tate Gallery, p. 12; Victoria and Albert Museum, pp. 14, 18, 22.

Every effort has been made to contact copyright holders of any material reproduced in this book. Any omissions will be rectified in subsequent printings if notice is given to the publisher.

Names in SMALL CAPS in the text are characters in the play.

Some words are shown in bold, **like this.**
You can find out what they mean by looking in the glossary.

CONTENTS

THE SOURCES OF ROMEO AND JULIET

William Shakespeare was a professional actor, a businessman, and a playwright. Today, nearly 400 years after his death, his plays are still performed, moving audiences to tears and to laughter. Shakespeare's works tell us much about **Elizabethan** England. What is most remarkable is that Shakespeare's plays can still tell us something about ourselves.

By 1594 or 1595, when the play *Romeo and Juliet* was probably written, Shakespeare had already begun to make his mark in the London theater scene. Back home in Stratford-upon-Avon, he had left behind a wife, whom he had married when he was eighteen, and three children. His eldest child, Susannah, was thirteen, about the same age as Juliet. Shakespeare was 30 years old. He was an experienced man, poised for success in what was still an exciting new form of entertainment—the theater.

Shakespeare had a shrewd understanding of the subjects that would be popular with audiences. That included the theme of tragic young love. A version of *Romeo and Juliet*, printed and sold in London in 1599, was described as "an excellent and lamentable **tragedy**. . . ." *Romeo and Juliet* was a success right from the start.

The story of Romeo and Juliet was well-known in several forms before Shakespeare made it his own. There had been poems, plays, and stories in Italian and in French. In 1567, William Painter had included "The goodly history of Rhomeo and Julietta" in a volume of short stories. Even earlier, in 1562, another writer, Arthur Brooke, had turned the story into a long poem titled "The Tragical History of Romeus and

THE
MOST EX-
cellent and lamentable
Tragedie, of Romeo
and *Iuliet*.

*Newly corrected, augmented, and
amended:*

As it hath bene sundry times publiquely acted, by the
right Honourable the Lord Chamberlaine
his Seruants.

LONDON
Printed by Thomas Creede, for Cuthbert Burby, and are to
be sold at his shop neare the Exchange.
1599.

The 1599 edition of the tragedy of Shakespeare's young lovers, Romeo and Juliet, was sure to be popular.

This illustration from 1616 shows a duel.

Juliet." There are similarities between Brooke's poem and Shakespeare's play. Shakespeare may even have had the poem in front of him as he wrote.

IMPROVING THE ORIGINALS

It was quite normal for Elizabethan playwrights to use existing stories as the basis for their plays. Shakespeare was a master at choosing the most interesting ideas and developing them into something more complex than the originals. In *Romeo and Juliet,* there is a wider range of attitudes toward love than in any of the stories on which it was based. MERCUTIO is full of brutal bravado. He mocks pretensions to romantic love. He is in marked contrast to ROMEO. But he is mentioned in only one line of Brooke's poem.

It may be said that Brooke's poem is rather dull. But Shakespeare turns it into a story of great contrasts. Right from the start there is a sense of dreadful fate. The lovers are doomed. But along the way, there is music, dancing, comedy, sword fights, and wit. The play is a wonderful piece of theater, full of action and energy.

Shakespeare's use of language is also more interesting. The contrasts in the play are expressed in many different styles. These range from formal poetry to witty puns, from the angry outbursts of Juliet's father to the passionate idealism of the lovers. The atmosphere of the play is felt through its language.

THE STAR-CROSSED LOVERS

The opening **Chorus** refers to Romeo and Juliet as "a pair of star-crossed lovers." This famous description conveys the brilliant intensity of their love, as well as the **tragedy** of their deaths. They fall in love at first sight and within a day they are married. Friar Laurence warns that love of such intensity cannot last long.

These violent delights have violent ends.

The two lovers often talk of each other as light or stars or sun. Romeo calls Juliet "the sun," "bright angel," "my soul." For her, he is like the stars.

Come, loving, black-browed night.
Give me my Romeo. And when I
shall die,
Take him and cut him out in little stars,
And he will make the face of heaven

so fine
That all the world will be in love
with night.

This is one of several moments when Juliet has a premonition of death. Bright light is the symbol of their love, but they are also aware that light is overshadowed by darkness and that eternal darkness means death.

As dawn breaks after their wedding night and Romeo must leave for Mantua, they say,

JULIET: O, now be gone! More light and light it grows.

ROMEO: More light and light: more dark and dark our woes.

Juliet dances with Capulet in the 1980 Royal Shakespeare Company production.

A DOOMED LOVE

The sense that their lives and love are doomed grows little by little, but, at the beginning of the play, both young people seem fortunate. Romeo's mother cares about him and is pleased he wasn't involved in the recent outbreak of violence between the families. Juliet's father seems loving and protective toward her. He tries to persuade her **suitor**, PARIS, that she is too young to marry. Juliet's house comes to life in the party her father has enjoyed organizing. When TYBALT recognizes Romeo, Capulet won't have him turned away, because he is "a virtuous and well-governed youth," not a troublemaker.

But such affection and good sense is fragile and short-lived. The reality of Juliet's life, and quickly Romeo's, too, is lonely and insecure. No other characters, least of all their parents, have anything like the honesty and faithfulness of the lovers. LADY CAPULET was married young herself and is only 28 years old. She has a cool relationship with both her husband and daughter. When Juliet appeals to her mother for help,

O sweet mother, cast me not away!

there is no sympathy in her mother's reply.

Talk not to me, for I'll not speak a word.
Do as thou wilt, for I have done with thee.

When even the NURSE thinks that Juliet should cut her losses, forget Romeo, and marry Paris, Juliet grows up quickly.

She must be responsible for her own decisions. She is prepared to die if all other plans fail.

Juliet's appeals for her parents' understanding are met with coolness in a 1994 German production.

VICTIMS OF CHANCE?

It could be said that ROMEO and JULIET die because of terrible, bad luck. FRIAR LAURENCE is their counselor and friend, but in the end, they are alone. Romeo is to endure banishment, and Juliet faces waking up in a tomb. They cannot even keep in contact with one another. Such total loneliness makes them very vulnerable. When things go horribly wrong and Romeo believes that Juliet is really dead, the Friar tries to save the situation. But he is too late.

Watching the play on stage, we feel that the story could work out differently. There are so many other possibilities. If only MERCUTIO had not been killed; if only Friar Laurence had used a better messenger; if only Juliet had woken up five minutes earlier. Our sense of mischance, or bad luck, is very strong in this play. In a good performance, it is

the painful sense of "if only" that makes us feel that this is indeed a tragic love story.

This is the famous balcony scene, where Romeo and Juliet vow true love and devotion to each other. This photograph is from a 1989 production.

A TRAGEDY OF TWO FAMILIES

Romeo and Juliet have been born into a world of violence and hate. As the only children of two powerful, constantly feuding families, they are caught up in a whirlwind of anger, insults, fighting, and death. New acts of violence keep them apart, even after they have declared their love. Their wretchedness lies in this isolation. What chance does a secret love have against organized hate? Romeo and Juliet are powerless. They are out-numbered and out-maneuvered.

In the end, the play is a **tragedy** not just of two young lovers, but also of two great families. The bitter outcome of the years of feuding is that the MONTAGUES and CAPULETS both lose their only children. The families are as doomed as Romeo and Juliet. In the final scene, they agree to end the violence and erect statues in memory of the dead lovers. But there is still a sense of shocking and irretrievable waste. As the Prince says,

A glooming peace this morning with it brings:
The sun for sorrow will not show his head . . .
For never was a story of more woe
Than this of Juliet and her Romeo.

Romeo grieves for Juliet. The audience feels sad and anxious because it knows there is more tragedy to come. This scene is from the 1992 Royal Shakespeare Company production.

THE CHARACTERS IN THE PLAY

ESCALUS Prince of Verona.

MERCUTIO Related to the Prince and a friend of Romeo.

PARIS A young nobleman, related to the Prince and Mercutio. He is in love with Juliet.

SERVANT TO COUNT PARIS

MONTAGUE The head of a family of Verona, feuding with the Capulets.

LADY MONTAGUE Montague's wife.

ROMEO The Montague's only child.

BENVOLIO Romeo's cousin and friend.

ABRAHAM Montague's servant.

BALTHASAR Romeo's servant.

CAPULET The head of a family of Verona, feuding with the Montagues.

LADY CAPULET His wife.

JULIET The Capulet's only child.

TYBALT Juliet's cousin.

AN OLD MAN of the Capulet family.

Romeo tries to calm things between his friend, Mercutio, and the Capulet, Tybalt. This scene is from Gielgud's production in 1935.

NURSE Juliet's nurse.

PETER A servant of the Capulet family.

Men of the Capulet household:
SAMPSON
GREGORY
ANTHONY
POTPAN
A CLOWN
A SERVANT

FRIAR LAURENCE A Franciscan **friar**. Romeo's friend and Juliet's helper.

FRIAR JOHN A Franciscan friar. Friar Laurence sends him to Mantua with a letter for Romeo.

AN **APOTHECARY** Living in Mantua. He supplies Romeo with poison.

Three Musicians:
SIMON CATLING
HUGH REBECK
JAMES SOUNDPOST

Members of the watch, citizens of Verona, dancers, **torchbearers**, **pages**, and servants.

CHORUS Opens the play. A character who plays no part in the story, but comments on it.

Before the **tragedy** unfolds, there is happy affection between Juliet and her nurse. This scene is from the 1992 Royal Shakespeare Company production.

WHAT HAPPENS IN THE PLAY

THE QUARREL

The young men of the Montague and Capulet families are at it again. Their long-standing feud has boiled over, and they are fighting in the street. ESCALUS, Prince of Verona, comes to break it up and orders a ban on fighting in the streets. If they cannot control themselves, he says, then he must do it for them.

ROMEO hasn't been involved this time. He's feeling miserable because he's in love with Rosaline. But Rosaline doesn't love him. His cousin BENVOLIO tells him to find another girl.

A QUESTION OF MARRIAGE

Meanwhile in the Capulet's house, the COUNT PARIS is asking to marry JULIET. He tells her father that at fourteen she is

not too young. CAPULET would prefer him to wait for two years, but eventually tells Paris to speak to Juliet. If she consents, then he will give his permission. Capulet invites Paris to a party he is giving that night. It will be a chance for him to meet Juliet.

BEFORE THE PARTY

Romeo and Benvolio hear about Capulet's party and that Rosaline will be there. They decide to attend the party uninvited. LADY CAPULET tells Juliet about Count Paris. Both she and Juliet's NURSE encourage Juliet to watch him at the party. Paris would be a fine catch, if she could love him as a husband.

THE PARTY

The party is in full swing when the Montagues arrive wearing masks so they won't be recognized. During a dance Romeo sees a girl. At once, Rosaline is forgotten. It is love at first sight.

Did my heart love till now?
Foreswear it, sight!
For I ne'er saw beauty till this night.

TYBALT, Juliet's cousin, recognizes Romeo as a Montague and wants to throw him out. Capulet, however, insists that the party should not be spoiled. He has heard good things about Romeo, who in any case isn't making trouble. But Tybalt is furious and is determined to get back at the Montagues later. Romeo manages to have a few moments alone with Juliet. He kisses her. The Nurse interrupts to call Juliet to her mother, and Romeo realizes that she is a Capulet and the daughter of the house. He leaves at once. The Nurse tells Juliet about Romeo. Juliet realizes that she's in an impossible position—she loves a family enemy.

Capulet's party is in full swing in this scene from the 1994 production at the Schauspielhous in Germany.

THE BALCONY SCENE

ROMEO's friends have lost him in the rush to get away from the party unharmed. They think he must be hiding nearby, so they make teasing remarks about ROSALINE. He doesn't answer, and they leave.

Romeo comes out of hiding and sees JULIET standing at her window. Coming nearer, he hears her speaking. She is talking about him and about how she loves him. They vow true love and devotion to each other.

Juliet suggests that they marry in secret. Their two families hate each other too much to allow them to make their love public. She will send a message to Romeo telling him where and when they can meet for the ceremony.

The NURSE calls Juliet inside, and reluctantly she goes. Romeo leaves to visit his friend **FRIAR** LAURENCE for advice and help.

FRIAR LAURENCE'S CELL

Romeo tells the friar how deeply in love he is with Juliet. Friar Laurence, remembering his young friend's infatuation with Rosaline—now so easily displaced—is not sure Romeo could be so deeply in love with Juliet so quickly. But Friar Laurence is hopeful that, if it is true love, then a marriage might heal the old feud between the families.

THE GO-BETWEEN

The Nurse is sent to find Romeo. She warns him not to deceive Juliet, but Romeo convinces her of his seriousness. She agrees to help Juliet find a way of going to Friar Laurence's **cell** that afternoon. It is there that the two lovers will be married. Juliet is impatient for news when the Nurse returns, but eventually learns of Romeo's plan. While she prepares for the visit to Friar Laurence for the marriage ceremony, the Nurse goes to find the ladder that will help Romeo climb up to Juliet's bedroom that night.

THE MARRIAGE CEREMONY

Juliet joins Romeo at Friar Laurence's cell, and the friar takes them off to be married.

Romeo (Sean Bean) and Juliet (Niamh Cusak) are united in marriage by Friar Laurence in the 1986 Royal Shakespeare Company production.

A Fight

Benvolio and Mercutio meet Tybalt and other Capulets. Tybalt is still looking for a fight with Romeo after the incident at the Capulet party, but Romeo, when he arrives, refuses to fight. He tries to calm things down by reminding everyone of the Prince's order. But Mercutio will not be stopped and takes up Tybalt's challenge. Romeo steps between the two friends, which results in a sword being thrust into Mercutio's body. Mercutio, badly wounded, blames Romeo for interfering, and he blames both families for the feud. Mercutio dies. When Tybalt returns, Romeo fights and kills him. Benvolio tells Romeo that Romeo will be held responsible if the Prince hears about the fight.

Almost at once the Prince arrives with the Montagues and the Capulets. Benvolio tells them what happened, and Lady Capulet demands that Romeo be executed. The Prince, however, seeing that Romeo was avenging the death of Mercutio, orders that Romeo be banished. He must leave Verona.

Banishment

Juliet is waiting impatiently for night when Romeo will come to her. The Nurse gives her the news of Tybalt's death and Romeo's punishment. Juliet is distraught. Meanwhile, **Friar** Laurence is bringing Romeo news of his banishment. Romeo cannot bear the thought of leaving Juliet. The Nurse now arrives to tell Romeo of Juliet's grief. Only Friar Laurence seems able to think straight, and he tells Romeo to

visit that night as planned. But Romeo must leave before dawn and go to Mantua, a distant city. Friar Laurence will try to reconcile the Montagues and Capulets with news of their children's marriage. Romeo can come back to be with Juliet after the friar has succeeded in reconciling the families.

A Marriage is Arranged

Count Paris, however, is still determined to marry Juliet. Her parents, numbed by the shock of Tybalt's death, and without consulting her, agree. Juliet and Paris will marry in three days' time.

The Lovers Part

Romeo and Juliet have spent their wedding night together. Dawn is breaking as Romeo leaves. Looking down on him from her balcony, Juliet imagines him in a tomb.

Juliet's mother now arrives to tell Juliet of her upcoming marriage to Paris. Shocked, Juliet answers plainly. No. She repeats this to her father who loses his temper and threatens to disown her if she disobeys. Neither her father nor her mother will listen to her, and Juliet turns to Nurse for help, but even she doesn't understand how much Juliet is in love. She tells Juliet to forget Romeo. He is banished and may never return. Juliet seems to agree and goes to Friar Laurence's **cell** to pray, she says, for forgiveness.

Romeo fights Tybalt and avenges the
death of Mercutio in the 1973 Royal
Shakespeare Company production.

At Friar Laurence's Cell

Paris is asking the **friar** to be ready to join himself and Juliet in marriage when Juliet arrives. When she is alone with the friar, Juliet tells him that she will kill herself rather than be unfaithful to Romeo. Friar Laurence, understanding her strength, outlines a daring plan. She is to go home and agree to marry Paris. The next night she must drink a special potion before going to sleep. The potion will make her appear to be dead. Her parents will bury her in the family tomb. Meanwhile, Friar Laurence will tell Romeo what is happening. Romeo will come back, go to the **tomb**, wake Juliet, and they will be reunited. Juliet agrees.

Preparing for a Wedding— and a Death

As the Capulets prepare the marriage feast, Juliet goes to her room. She is afraid of waking up in the tomb before Romeo arrives, and she is afraid that the potion won't work. In that case, she will stab herself to death rather than marry Paris. Finally, thinking of Romeo, she drinks the potion.

The Death Discovered

Juliet is found "dead" on her wedding morning. Her parents, Nurse, and Paris are overcome by grief. The friar takes charge. Juliet is buried without delay in the family tomb.

The Plan Goes Wrong

Romeo's servant, Balthasar, returns to Mantua from Verona with tragic news. He has seen Juliet lowered into the tomb. Convinced she is dead, Romeo finds poison and goes back to Verona to kill himself at Juliet's grave.

Friar Laurence has sent Friar John with a letter to Romeo, in which the apparent death of Juliet is explained. But Friar John is not allowed into Mantua. The authorities think he is carrying the **plague.** When Friar Laurence realizes that Romeo has not been given the message, he goes to Juliet's tomb. He will be there when she wakes and hide her in his **cell** until Romeo can be brought to Verona.

At Juliet's Grave

Paris and his servant come to the tomb. Hearing someone, Paris hides. It is Romeo and Balthasar. Balthasar is given a letter to take to Romeo's father and is sent away. Instead of leaving, he hides nearby. Paris is outraged when Romeo begins to open Juliet's tomb. He leaps at Romeo. There is a fight, and Paris is killed. Paris's servant runs to get help. Romeo opens the tomb, says a last goodbye to Juliet, and drinks the poison. He falls dead at her side.

Friar Laurence and Balthasar now come to the tomb. They find the bodies of Paris and Romeo just as Juliet wakes. The Friar, afraid for his own safety, urges Juliet to leave, but she stays behind. Alone, she kills herself with Romeo's dagger.

TOGETHER IN DEATH

Paris's servant has brought help. Balthasar and Friar Laurence have been brought back to the tomb. The PRINCE, the Capulets, and the Montagues arrive. Friar Laurence tells the tragic story of the young lovers. The two fathers, united by grief, agree to end their feud.

For never was a story of more woe
Than this of Juliet and her Romeo.

The is the final scene from the 1961 Royal Shakespeare Company production. Romeo and Juliet lie together in death, and their families are united in grief.

DIRECTORS' PERSPECTIVES

By the end of the nineteenth century, theater-goers had very strong ideas about what the two lovers should be like. The characters had taken root in the popular imagination. This century, the greatest actors and directors have risen to the challenge of the play. Far from wishing to imitate famous productions of the past, they have tried to make each new production fresh. There have been some famous experiments—a popular movie version directed by Franco Zeffirelli; a highly dramatic 1940 ballet danced to music by Prokofiev; and Leonard Bernstein and Stephen Sondheim's 1957 musical, *West Side Story.*

In 1934, the actor-director John Gielgud put together a talented company for a production in which he and Laurence Olivier alternated the parts of ROMEO and MERCUTIO. Gielgud was brilliant at understanding Shakespeare's language. He could shape a speech and phrase a line to make sense and to reveal the rhythm and beauty of the poetry. Other actors in the company learned from him, and the performance had conviction, pace, and energy.

Gielgud was especially successful with the verbal wit of Mercutio, while Olivier was more passionate as Romeo. Peggy Ashcroft was praised as "the finest JULIET of our time." As another said of the lovers played by Olivier and Ashcroft,

Larry (Olivier) to me was the Romeo. . . . They've really got to be in love, these kids.

In John Gielgud's production of the play in 1935, his Mercutio (right) was particularly successful, while Laurence Olivier portrayed a more passionate Romeo. Edith Evans played the NURSE.

The play has been so frequently performed in the twentieth century that several leading actors have appeared in more than one production and passed on insights from earlier work. Edith Evans, an outstanding character actress, played the Nurse in the 1930s with Ashcroft, Olivier, and Gielgud. She played the role again as a very old woman at Stratford-upon-Avon in 1961. Experience of the world was ingrained in each line of her face. Her extraordinarily flexible, deep voice could still break into a chuckle of pleasure. The director, Peter Hall, used her age and experience as a contrast to a touchingly young Juliet, played by Dorothy Tutin. The bond between them was very strong. The moment when they no longer feel the same and Juliet is really alone was extremely sad.

In 1976, another young director, Trevor Nunn, assembled a strong cast for his Royal Shakespeare Company production at Stratford. In the early stages of rehearsal, he asked the actors to think back to their own adolescence. They were given homework.

- Do you remember your first adult love affair or kiss? Write something down about who, where, and maybe what you felt.
- Write down the most extremely violent thing you have done in your life.
- Write down a little story about any feud you have known.

This process meant that the actors were using feelings they remembered from their own young lives. Their performances were strong and convincing as a result.

Edith Evans returned to the role of Nurse nearly 30 years later under the direction of Peter Hall. Dorothy Tutin played Juliet. This photograph is from the 1961 production.

Michael Bogdanov directed *Romeo and Juliet* five times in twenty years. He developed views on how to make plays written 400 years ago relevant for today. One very significant step was the switch to modern dress, which he first used in a performance in 1976. The actors wore costumes of the **Elizabethan** period for most of the play. Then in the last scene, staged as if it were a press conference, two gold statues, erected in memory of the two families' dead children, were unveiled. The actors wore modern dress for this scene. Some members of the audience left confused and disgusted at this break with tradition. Others were excited by a final moment that brought the issues of the play up-to-date.

Bogdanov explains that with modern dress, an audience can pick up information about the characters, just as we do in ordinary life. For example, the text of the play suggests that MONTAGUE is of higher social status than CAPULET. The audience realizes this at a glance if Montague is dressed in a tailored, expensive, designer suit and Capulet is dressed in an off-the-rack, department store suit.

In 1989 a production of *Romeo and Juliet* visited a number of towns in England. The whole theater—lighting, seating, stage, costumes, and so on—was packed into four 44-foot (13 meters) trucks in one town on a Saturday night and unpacked in another on Sunday. The staging was set up in a large hall, and the production was ready for its first audience on Monday night. Many members of these audiences had seen very few theater performances before this one.

Michael Bogdanov's modern-dress production in 1986 had TYBALT (Hugh Quarshie) styled as a leather-clad biker.

The director of the touring company, Terry Hands, and the designer, Farrah, had clear ideas about their goals. They wanted to encourage an intimate relationship between what was happening on stage and the people in the audience. They wanted the performance to be powerful and direct. To help this, they used a thrust stage, a long rectangular platform that puts the audience on three sides, so that everyone was close to the action. They kept scenery to a minimum because they didn't want people to be distracted from the language of the play. They used simple lighting to create atmosphere, including dappled light to suggest moonlight through leaves beneath JULIET's balcony and just a shaft of light as from a lantern in the darkness of the tomb. The lighting for the daytime street scenes suggested the extreme heat of Italy. And the personalities were exaggerated. For example, the NURSE positively enjoyed the jokes and teasing done her at her expense, and MERCUTIO was dangerous and explosive.

Shakespeare has put so much into his plays it is like a multifaceted diamond. Any production team, if they are lucky, might get half of them.

(Farrah, designer)

Tim McInnerny plays Mercutio in a 1991 production.

ACTORS' PERSPECTIVES

JULIET

Peggy Ashcroft, the JULIET of her generation in the 1930s, had this to say about playing Juliet:

*I see Romeo and Juliet as in themselves the most glorius, life-giving people. What you have to take into account is their ages. She is a girl of 14, ROMEO is a boy of 16. I discovered in playing her that the essential thing is youth rather than being tragic. I think she's a victim of circumstance. The **tragedy** is simply something that happens to her.*

Georgina Slowe played Juliet in Terry Hands' 1989 touring production. The great quality of her performance was youthfulness. She was in her early twenties, but, with long dark hair and simple, flowing costumes, the audience could believe that she was only in her teens. Her quick, light movements and liveliness added even more to this impression.

Peggy Ashcroft played Juliet to John Gielgud's Romeo in the 1930s. Ashcroft saw Juliet as a youthful "victim of circumstance" rather than as a tragic heroine.

In a discussion with a group of students after the performance, Georgina Slowe described the work she had done to find her fourteen-year-old self. She still had diaries she had written at that age, and she read them again to remind herself of how it felt to be fourteen.

Claire Holman played Juliet in 1992 in Stratford-upon-Avon and in London. She and her director, David Leveaux, were fascinated by the way Romeo talks about her in an almost religious way. She is his "soul," his good angel, his guiding star.

Any actress playing Juliet is faced with a great acting challenge. She must recreate a young girl who falls deeply in love, but who is overcome by serious and frightening problems. Isolated from her family, she must face agonizing decisions with extraordinary bravery and sense of purpose.

Claire Holman and Michael Maloney play Romeo and Juliet in Leveaux's 1992 production. The balcony symbolizes their love. It is fragile, and Romeo has to struggle to reach it.

In the 1992 production, Claire Holman had to show yet another dimension— the spiritual bond between Juliet and the banished Romeo. Juliet's balcony was simply a fragile platform suspended high out of reach. The actor playing Romeo, Michael Maloney, had a real physical challenge to reach her. Later in the performance, Claire Holman was suspended high above the stage to hover over Romeo in Mantua, as if she were a vision inspiring him.

ROMEO

On stage ROMEO is often understood most clearly as a contrast to the other young men, particularly MERCUTIO. In Gielgud's production of 1934, he and Laurence Olivier alternated the roles. They understood the difference between the two characters very well.

One of Michael Bogdanov's spectacular modern-dress productions put a sports car on stage, dressed TYBALT, Prince of Cats played by Hugh Quarshie, in black biker's leather, and made Mercutio, played by Michael Kitchen, a cool and quietly dangerous fellow. Against this macho world, Romeo, played by Sean Bean was much more open and sensitive and the only one capable of falling in love.

In Terry Hand's 1989 production, Mark Rylance's Romeo began as a changeable personality affected by the mood of people around him. He begins to act like them, too. Mercutio, played by David O'Hara, was viciously witty, contemptuous of any hint of gentleness or idealism, which he saw as ridiculous. The cynicism of this Mercutio was so extreme that it suggested some hidden pain being covered up.

Romeo was responsive to Mercutio's moods and the audience could sense that he understood his friend's deeper feelings. But Romeo also had an introverted side which led him to spend time alone. When he met JULIET, it was as if he had found a soul mate at last. All his sensitivity and gentleness took over. Juliet rapidly gains the maturity to go her own way, and Romeo, too, grows up when he falls in love.

The gentle character of Romeo (actor Laurence Olivier, third from right) is often in contrast to the explosive Mercutio (John Gielgud, second from right). This scene is taken from Gielgud's 1935 production.

THE NURSE

Any actress cast as the NURSE is presented with a range of choices. She begins as JULIET's closest friend. She is more of a mother to her than LADY CAPULET. But while she has a lively personality and can share Juliet's experiences as a friend, she fails to understand the depth of Juliet's feeling for Romeo. She lets Juliet down. The actress must think this through in detail and understand the Nurse's views.

When Edith Evans played the Nurse as a very old woman, the Nurse fails Juliet because of the age gap. The comforting, happy affection between them was something Juliet had to leave behind when she was propelled into adult responsibility. This Nurse couldn't understand Juliet's predicament because the girl's high principles were so very far from her own priorities of old age. Nurse was looking for security and comfort, and for things to stay the same. Inevitably she and Juliet were finally separated by their different perspectives on life.

In 1989, Sheila Reid was a lively, middle-aged Nurse with an earthy zest for life. When she advised Juliet to forget Romeo and marry PARIS, she revealed that her true feelings, being true to inner principles, meant less to her than securing a good position in the world. As Juliet's Nurse, she would have had a role in the new household. Sheila Reid managed to make the audience feel that, while she and Juliet had no chance of successfully disobeying the men in authority in their lives, she still regretted that things had to be that way.

In contrast with Tybalt's leather and Mercutio's business suit, Romeo's soft outfit in Bogdanov's 1986 production emphasized sensitivity and openness.

SHARKS, JETS, AND ANIMATED TALES

One of the most successful modern recreations of *Romeo and Juliet* is the musical *West Side Story*. It was written in 1957, with music by the American composer and conductor Leonard Bernstein. Lyrics were by Stephen Sondheim, who has also written many other popular musicals. A few years later, *West Side Story* was made into a movie directed by Robert Wise and Jerome Robbins. The movie won the Academy Award for Best Film in 1961.

Since it was made, the movie has been seen all around the world. The stage musical has been produced time and again by professional companies, amateur groups, and school groups. Shakespeare's play has come to life for thousands of late twentieth-century school children through the brilliant work of Bernstein and Sondheim and the superb **choreography** of Jerome Robbins.

Together, they translated the play into modern language and brought it up-to-date. Verona becomes New York. The Montagues and Capulets become the warring street gangs of the Sharks and the Jets. JULIET is a Puerto Rican girl named Maria. She is not allowed to mix with Jet boys, but she falls in love with one of them anyway.

In the musical *West Side Story*, Shakespeare's warring families of medieval Italy are replaced by New York City street gangs, and Juliet's balcony becomes an apartment building fire escape.

The many school productions in the 1960s and 1970s encouraged teachers to be bold in exploring Shakespeare in school. They found issues and emotions that are still interesting today. Gradually a more demanding young audience for Shakespeare developed. This in turn encouraged directors, such as Bogdanov, to find exciting ways of communicating.

In fact, the medium of film is helping to create an appetite for Shakespeare in even younger children. In 1993, six of the plays became animated stories for television. Each one used a different technique of animation. *Romeo and Juliet* was shown as a romantic fairy tale. In the animated retelling of the story, great emphasis was placed on the beauty of the medieval Italian setting and on the blossoming of young love.

Like all the animated tales, Shakespeare's play was reduced to only twenty minutes. However, the essence of the story was successfully captured, and it is already proving to be a good introduction to the play for a wide range of people.

In the 1800s, there often seemed to be an ideal, and rather sentimental, picture of *Romeo and Juliet*. All actual productions were measured against this ideal.

Twentieth-century actors, directors, and those who have recreated the play in a new medium, have brought to light the toughness of the play. They have shown that young love must make hard decisions, and that all too often it is doomed by the violence of society. The **tragedy** of Romeo and Juliet is also the tragedy of the Montagues and the Capulets. It is the tragedy of any divided, violent society, including the society of today.

Romeo and Juliet shows the damage that divided, violent societies can have on individual lives. This is a scene from the 1976 production at The Other Place in Stratford-upon-Avon, England.

GLOSSARY

apothecary druggist or pharmacist

cell small room in a monastery

choreography planning of movements for dance performances

chorus in ancient Greek drama, a group of performers who observe, comment on, and sometimes participate in the action of the play

Elizabethan relating to Queen Elizabeth I of England and her reign, from 1533–1603

friar man who belongs to a brotherhood of the Roman Catholic church

go-between person who goes back and forth between others with messages

members of the watch those who guard and protect

page youth who attends to a person of high rank

plague also called bubonic plague, a highly infectious disease transmitted by fleas that live on rats

suitor man who is dating or wishes to date a woman

tomb place of burial above ground for a dead body

torchbearer person who carries a torch

tragedy form of play that shows the downfall of a hero and the suffering and death that the downfall creates

MORE BOOKS TO READ

Burdett, Lois. *Romeo & Juliet For Kids.* Buffalo, NY: Firefly Books, Limited, 1998.

Claybourne, Anna and Rebecca Treays. *World of Shakespeare.* Tulsa, Okla: E D C Publishing, 1997.

Ganeri, Anita. *Young Person's Guide to Shakespeare.* San Diego, Calif.: Harcourt, 1999.

Hort, John and Leela Hort (eds.) *Romeo & Juliet: The Inessential Shakespeare.* Studio City, Calif.: Empire Publishing Service, 1992.

Shakespeare, William. *The Tragedy of Romeo & Juliet.* Nashua, N.H.: Mesa View, Incorporated. 1999.

Stanley, Diane. *The Bard of Avon.* New York: Morrow, William & Company, Incorporated, 1998.

ADDITIONAL RESOURCES

African-American Shakespeare Company
5214-F Diamond Heights Blvd.
PMB 923
San Francisco, CA 94131
Tel: (415) 333-1918
This company's mission is to produce European classical works with an African-American cultural perspective

The Shakespeare Theatre
516 8th Street SE
Washington, DC 20003
(202) 547-3230
One of the top Shakespeare companies in the U.S., its mission is to produce and preserve classical theater and to develop new audiences for classical theater.

INDEX